The Unwoven Self

A Study in Self-Honesty

Khushboo Sheth

BookLeaf
Publishing

India | USA | UK

Made with ❤ on the BookLeaf Publishing Platform
www.bookleafpub.in
www.bookleafpub.com

Dedication

To Mom, Dad, and my brother, Ishaan.

For what holds steady when everything changes.

To myself, and to Life.

For what keeps changing, no matter what I do.

Preface

This book is not about discovering the meaning of life.

This book is about discovering that meaning can be assigned and you can pretty much get away with convincing people of your version if you sound confident enough.

Think of it as a field report from someone who tried to make sense of life, tripped over her own thoughts, and decided to write it down before forgetting the good bits.

These poems examine universal human experiences like doubt, faith, uncooperative kitchen appliances, and vague, persistent, almost annoying hope.

If there's a philosophy here, it's this: *You will be okay as long as you're honest with yourself, and keep drinking tea, I guess.*

Acknowledgements

Gratitude to everyone who contributed to this collection (whether intentionally or by accident).

And to the **_universe_**, for its remarkable ability to create chaos and call it inspiration.

1. Where Truth Lives

The right judgement
lies between mercy and justice
where compassion meets accountability,
and being human means knowing both.

What must be done
lies between word and deed,
a narrow pathway of intention,
definite and ungiving.

The right time to act
lies between life and death
where hesitation and consequence
share the same breath.

And, maybe, the peace we seek
lies in the space between
what's done and what we mean,
between the storm outside
and the one within.

2. Let the Song Remain

I heard a song when I was young, a tune half fragile, half
profound.
I moved with it till the night was done, as if I'd
remembered a long-lost sound.

The song played low and said to me,
*"Some things fade before their time, Some things are
carved in certainty."*

Years went by, the song returned, at every crossroad
worth a name.
Sometimes it spoke of things I'd earned, sometimes of
loss and guilt and blame.

It played when I learned that kindness costs so much
more than it should.
It played again when I learned that I'd still choose it if I
could.

It played when I was truly happy, when things were

finally falling into place.
It played soft, and it played steady, when it was my time
to fall from grace.

The song still plays again, again; Each time I lose, each
time I gain,
Each time I praise, each time I complain, until I have to
find myself again.

Now every note recalls a time, a fault or a deliberate
choice.
Each verse finds its rhythm and rhyme; Each word finds
meaning in the noise.

And yet I wish I could hear the song, just the tune, the
chords played plain,
Strip them of every memory and meaning,
and let the song remain.

3. Mastery

It started as a spark, a twitch,
or maybe just the need to know.
A fascination with the art,
a pull to see how deep I'd go.

I learned a hundred obscure things,
for answers to unasked questions,
I painted, read, and tried to write,
dissected every lesson.

Each effort seemed without a goal,
an unknown trail, an endless path.
No plan, no purpose, no clear line,
just practice for an unseen art.

Each brushstroke called for precision,
each page revealed a hidden fire,
each language lent a different lens,
each inkblot in itself a choir.

For the longest time I thought I sought
the skill itself, the craft, the mark.
But every work, in truth, was that,
a study not of hand, but heart.

And now I see what I was after,
the truth behind each restless call,
the work was never for word or song,
it was to master myself all along.

4. The Red Kettle

I have an odd companion:
a kettle, red and chipped,
that whistles on tired mornings
when I stare blankly at the stove
before another job interview.

This kettle screams in the quiet of the night
as I try to gather my thoughts
into something resembling poetry.

This kettle sings in the mountains,
on some long-earned morning of peace,
the sound of it rising through thin air
as if to remind me that the world is big

This kettle gurgles when I'm crying,
when the world feels sharp and unkind,
when I no longer know where I belong.

The kettle hisses when I'm angry,

when unfairness stings,
and I'm learning once more
how to compose myself.

This kettle hums when I'm with my family,
candles lit, power gone,
voices weaving over laughter and warmth.

This kettle sighs when I am alone,
thinking of who I've been,
and who I'm trying to be.

This kettle still has much to see,
to murmur, howl, and tremble.
To serve, to soothe, to comfort me,
In all ways small and gentle.
I'm eager for what lies ahead,
for what this kettle's song will be
in the moments still unwritten,
it will share with me.

5. Floor 12A

It seemed a strange thing, looking back,
to change a name, to hide the crack,
the thirteenth floor became 12A,
as if that made the fear go away.

The elevator hummed in orange glow,
Its steel walls cold, its movement slow.
I searched for Floor 13, couldn't see,
the concierge then said quietly,

"Number 13 brings bad luck, miss,
so people learn to live like this."
"It's still the thirteenth floor, though, right?"
He smiled, "Yes, it helps them sleep at night."

And now I wonder, grown and still,
how many names I bend at will.
How often I have called attention, 'care',
or silence, 'peace', that isn't there.

How often laziness was 'self-care',
and bearing insults 'being fair'.
How often truth stood in disguise,
a Floor 12A beneath my lies.

We rename what we fear to see,
and hope the label sets us free.
We've all lived life on floor 12A,
some day, maybe, we'll press 13.

6. Driving in the Rain

The rain blurs lines the world once drew,
the streetlights melt in golden streams.
I drive through shades of emerald hue,
that turn the roads to enchanted dreams.

A thousand sparks, a spectral view,
the city hums in hidden themes.
It isn't light that makes it true,
nor rain that grants its mystic seams.

It's in how the gaze forgets its view,
and lets the mind dissolve extremes.
The heart, when softened, humbly deems
the magic lives within the seams.

So learn to blur, to loosen schemes,
to find what wonder might attune.
The world will shine in quiet dreams,
when seen beneath a silver moon.

7. What Life Owes Us

We tally kindness, weigh our pain,
as if the world keeps score.
We wait for praise to ease the strain,
as if we're owed something more.

We call on luck to find our name,
for love to see us through,
but life has never made that claim,
nor promised what we're due.

We pray our efforts earn accord,
our worry earns relief,
that virtue is its own reward,
that fairness mends our grief.

But here's the secret, listen close,
what you seek is not that far.
The hardest faith you'll ever keep
is faith in who you are.

So give yourself the strength you seek,
the grace, the heart, the might.
You'll see that every tool you need
was hiding in plain sight.

For joy and courage are self-bestowed,
not treasures on higher shelves.
Maybe life owes us nothing
we do not owe ourselves.

8. Nothing Personal

A few hours before sunrise,
I sat beside Fate.

She said she went by many names:
destiny, chance, coincidence,
life, kismet, providence.

Her smile was patient,
her eyes indifferent,
as if the future were no concern of hers.

I asked, "Why do you do what you do?"
I heard the edge in my own voice.

She looked almost surprised.
"Oh, it's nothing personal," she said.
"When people go off-track,
I nudge them back."

Then she tilted her head, curious.

"Now that you've asked me something,
I get to ask you one."

"What is it like to...to feel?" she asked.

"You don't know what it means to feel?"
I questioned. "And you decide people's lives?"

"I don't decide," she said.
"I influence.
Feeling would cloud my judgment."

I smiled. "It might improve it."

She paused.
Her eyes, glinting shards of glass.

"Did it improve yours?" she asked.

And I fell silent.

9. Not All Wisdom Comes from the Wise

They say it is the mark of the wise
to stay composed through strife;
a steady voice, a tempered heart,
no ire, no outrage, a placid life.

"Temper your soul, let anger die,
make sure it leaves no mark.
Bury the flame before it grows,
for anger only feeds the dark."

But which is worse, I sometimes ask:
false calm or rightful rage?
Why gift us anger, fierce and vast,
Then bind it in a cage?

Perhaps it was meant to play
the villain, the fool, the foe;
It spoke true when silence failed,
it burned to keep us whole.

If anger is not sage, not wise,
though clean, though true, though just,
then may the world belong to fools,
who speak when silence rusts.

For calm in the face of what is wrong
deserves no saintly prize.
I've learned that truth offends as much as lies;
Not all wisdom comes from the wise.

10. The Wrong Kind of God

It's true we must trust what we know,
the voice within, the self we show.
For when the world turns sharp or odd,
we are our own divining rod.

But fear and guilt, and envy's hue,
can shape the lies we think are true.
And pride, when clothed in reason's robes,
can shred to pieces our deepest hopes.

For trust in the self without a doubt
is blindness turned inside out.
And doubt in the self without true trust
turns all the years lived into dust.

Perhaps the holiest thing we can do
is question what we think is true,
to see where logic stands as fraud,
lest blind certainty crown the wrong kind of god.

11. The Desert Knows

Four wizened men sat by the desert flame,
their velvet coats in restless sway.
The wind and sand, like kindred souls,
whispered the secrets of the night away.

The sky was drenched in violet gold,
a splendid, star-encrusted dome.
A single firefly that lost its way,
was seeking heaven far from home.

The first one spoke, his voice was low,
"I offered comfort that would endure.
She turned away, I still don't know;
all it did was leave her future unsure."

The second stirred the glowing sand,
"I gave her rank, a place, a name.
and still she fled, as if carefree,
from crowns that others sought in vain."

The third one sighed, "I offered relief,
a quiet world, release from pain.
She took one look and sought the east
as if the storm was worth the strain."

The fourth one cupped the firefly,
its fragile light against his palm.
"I offered warmth. She wanted growth,
even if it burned her calm."

And there they sat till morning broke,
the wind grown still, the fire blue,
the firefly gone, the desert spoke:
Perhaps she only wanted what felt true.

12. Things that Don't Exist

They build their gods from evidence, from logic's
sharpened blade,
and doubt all that cannot be seen or heard or neatly
weighed.

They hold the world in measured hands, insist on what
exists,
yet miss the threads that hold it whole, through aeons
that persist.

The spark that lights a speaker's eyes, when passion
finds its flame,
no law can chart, nor truth deny, that force that has no
name.

That strange, unspoken calm that knows when life is at
its worst,
how order waits behind the storm to heal what chaos
cursed.

The child who stares as if aware of things beyond our
sight,
a wisdom waits behind that gaze, too ancient and too
bright.

The sea that hears our grief at night and answers with its
waves,
knows all we've lost, yet holds it close in watery,
wordless graves.

A flower blooms where none have been, thriving in the
barren cold;
proof lives beyond our search for *'seen'*, in the picture
seen as whole.

So weigh your truths and name your laws, define what
you insist,
but think, when your measures pause, *of things that
don't exist.*

13. The Raconteur

What if our goal was simply this: to gather tales to tell,
to live in moments, small and swift, and learn to see
them well.

A stranger on the morning bus, still talking on the
phone,
of how he missed his usual one, his schedule
overthrown.

A crumpled paper on the road, half written, half erased,
a writer paused mid-sentence there, still fighting through
the haze.

A voice that echoes late at night, a challenge through the
air,
two friends who race on empty roads with wind
entangled hair.

A girl with nail-paint on one hand, the other left
halfway,

proof beauty waits for no one's plan, nor what they have
to say.

A man in a brand-new suit, nervous, with *'tilak'* on his
head,
his mother's prayer still faintly seen in that bright
crimson red.

The ants that walk their sugarless trail, though all
reward is gone,
still march with faith, the scent won't fail, "still move,
still carry on".

A light that burns at 3 a.m., a desk, a shadowed face,
a student chasing some small dream through silence and
through grace.

And maybe that is all we need, to see and listen well,
just countless lives we meet and keep,
enough stories to tell.

14. "It Is What It Is"

They say it soft to dull the sting,
as if surrender is grace,
a phrase to hide from consequence,
a mask for their own face.

"It is what it is," they like to say,
and hide their hands from the fight,
but doing nothing wrong, sometimes,
still isn't doing right.

Acceptance has its time and place,
when all is tried and done,
but saying it too soon is sin
disguised as moving on.

I've seen a single act restore
what reason had dismissed,
so, don't declare it done
while breath and will persist.

For while there's one small chance to change,
one truth yet to exist,
we can't yet call it fate
and say, "it is what it is."

Though I see why we do.

15. The Strange Tenacity

A wildflower splits the concrete path, and blooms where
boots have pressed;
no sunlight promised, yet it grows, uninvited,
unaddressed.

A frog slows down to almost death, its body made of
stone,
and still, it wakes when winter ends, remembering its
own.

A fly keeps hammering at the glass, convinced the sky's
behind,
it fails, retreats, and flies again, rebelling against design.

A butterfly with paper wings outflies the mountain's
cold,
and crosses seas on borrowed winds, small, fearless,
uncontrolled.

An earthworm cut by garden blades grows back, resumes

its quest,
it doesn't rage, just exists, it knows that's what it does
best.

In ocean depths with no sunlight, where crushing
shadows press,
a fish invents its spark of blue glow, its small defiant
'yes'.

Leeches cling with tireless faith, through movement,
burn, and fear,
they simply hold until they must, their purpose crystal
clear.

I remember this, when the day is done, when effort feels
like myth,
and marvel at the strange tenacity existence is born with.

16. Forty-Two

It was a Saturday afternoon,
the kind that makes you forget what waiting feels like.
I sat on a park bench with a book,
nothing urgent, nothing owed.

The breeze moved slow through the trees.
Somewhere, a child laughed;
somewhere else, someone shouted into their phone.
The world carried on.

Then a rustle nearby. Faint, deliberate.
A baby crawled through the grass toward me,
its palms green, its knees brown,
its face bright with effort and discovery.
No parent in sight.
I looked up, called out,
heard nothing but the soft, ongoing day.
So I picked it up, sat it beside me.

It gurgled, clapped, reached for my book,

and with one damp hand
pressed a green print on page forty-two,
right on the word '*life*'.

I laughed, quietly, at the coincidence.
Of course it would be that page.
Of course it would be that word.

A woman appeared, breathless, relieved,
called the baby's name, gathered it close.
The world resumed its pattern.

I brushed the page, closed the book,
and sat a while longer,
thinking of how sometimes
meaning shows up uninvited,
asks for nothing,
and leaves before you can thank it.

17. You Can't Win All Wars

I knew, in the abstract, that toasters shouldn't matter
when there are wars.
My head agreed; my body lagged behind.

The toast lay in the slot like a tiny defeated thing, black
at the edges, soft in the centre.
The toaster didn't care. The toast didn't care. I did.

It would have been forgivable if it were the morning's
only crime.
But the microwave, in its quiet bureaucracy, returned hot
bowl and cold food.

This small betrayal pushed me further toward an absurd
edge.
So I surrendered: today, tea only.

I turned the kettle on.
It gurgled, then gargled, and boiled over.

I turned it off before it finished its sentence, and, defeated, I called in sick to work.

18. A Small Price to Pay

Headlights flash through tunnel walls,
I drive too fast, the engine calls.
The road hums low, the heart in tune,
the speed feels honest, sharp, immune.

A puzzle sprawled across my desk,
the pattern wrong, the logic, a mess.
Then one small piece slides into place,
and order lays chaos to rest.

A stranger lies with practiced ease,
I let them think they've fooled my peace.
There's pleasure in that quiet game,
the knowing, not the need to name.

I drink from cups brought far from here,
the clay holds heat, the taste feels clear.
The glaze remembers foreign hands,
the colour shifts, the light expands.

An author lost to time and trade,
his book half-torn, the words half-fade.
But one sharp line hits the nail on the head,
and something wakes, only asleep, not dead.

A kitten follows, sits, then goes.
It leaves its warmth upon the place it chose.
That small exchange, unasked, unseen
reminds me what alive can mean.

These moments flare and fade away,
too brief, too bright, too much to stay.
yet I would take them all and say:

If I get to meet a different self every day,
The trouble is a small price to pay.

19. The Illusion of Usefulness

Some learn tongues no one speaks,
trace lost sounds for quiet weeks.
They write their notes by candle's glow,
for words no living voice will know.

Some weave their rugs by hand, not trade,
each knot a promise, self-contained.
No factory could match the feel
of threads aligned to something real.

Some mix their colours from the ground,
though none will last once light's unbound.
They paint, then watch their work decay,
it's proof value isn't meant to stay.

Some cook for few when crowds would pay,
each plate exact, then cleared away.
They chase the balance, taste, and heat,
not profit, only what feels complete.

Some map the stars from city skies,
their day jobs plain, their nights precise.
They'll never touch the things they chart,
but still they learn each name by heart.

We ask what such labours earn,
what's gained for all the time we burn.
But maybe usefulness is just disguise,
a lens too small for wonder's size.

20. Why Poets Love the Moon

Poets love the moon, it's true,
an idol they keep writing through.
It borrows light, as poets do,
and weaves it with the silver dew.

It pulls at tides it cannot see,
yet shapes the shore, inevitably.
So too their words, each ebb and swell,
unnoticed, till they start to tell.

For creatures winged or ocean-bound,
the moon decides when paths are found.
It guides the flight, the course, the tune,
and poets, too, move by the moon.

The world admires the moon's display,
but wouldn't trade its sunlit day.
Just as they quote the poet's line,
but never wish the same design.

For like the moon, the poet learns,
to shine on what he'll never burn.
And bear the praise, and bear the cost,
of lighting paths they'll never cross.

21. On Hope

I kept looking for a reason to hope.
Something to justify it, to earn it.

But hope isn't reasonable.
It doesn't wait to be invited.

It just shows up when everything else leaves.

I tried to make sense of hope.
To find what it was built on.

Turns out it isn't built on anything.
That's why it survives.